SHE LEADS WITH HER HEART

MUSINGS ON LOVE, RELATIONSHIPS, AND TRUTH

MEGAN SAINT-MARIE

Some of these poems, in whole or in part, were previously published in Trestle Ties Digital Magazine 2021 and The Art of Being Human volume 15 Compiled & Edited by Daniela Voice and Brian Wrixon, Brian Wrixon Books

ISBN Paperback 979-8-9988579-0-4

ISBN Hardback 979-8-9988579-1-1

ISBN Ebook Version 979-8-9988579-2-8

CONTENTS

PREFACE

"I challenge you to get up in front people and read your work", she dared me.

That one sentence lead me to share my words, become slightly less scared, get published, read on the radio, and not care so much about what other people think.

It was the curve in a path that has allowed this self-proclaimed introvert to feel less weird and more courageous.

This book is a series of moments, some personal, and some merely observed.

I chose to write these in free verse, so leaving out commas and periods was an intentional, artistic choice.

I. EARLY YEARS

SEATTLE

Cold
    gray
    misty rain
    Simon and Garfunkel in the living room
    Dancing with dad
    and tambourines
    Feeling complete trust and safety
    The beige house with its Japanese paper doors off the bedroom
    the basement where dad set up old airplane control panels for us
to pretend we can fly through space
    Green and pink hula-hoops discarded on the grass out back
    as we run inside for dinner
    Shades of mist still mean love decades later
    the song playing should be called
    Hello Grayness My Old Friend
    as we sit down and watch the rain hit the windowpanes in big
gloppy drops

LAKE COWICHAN'S GURU

Why do they think he's so great
    He smells like smoke
    and old people
    and his dress is dirty
    I can't understand his accent
    his fingers are wrinkled and stained yellow
    with long dirty fingernails
    Gross
    Tonight we are all eating at the long wooden table for his
birthday
    The adults are talking baby talk
    and drinking wine out of baby bottles
    it's embarrassing
    I'm glad my friends from school aren't here
    how pathetic
    My brother and I walk home down the path
    to our tiny cabin
    Ghosts come

to dance their mischief stomp
That actually
feels less weird than dinner did

SUMMER CAMP, OR, I LEARNED MORE THAN HOW TO RIDE A HORSE

When I was eight my parents informed me that
    I was going to summer camp
    I protested to no avail
    They declared there were horses
    and by the way
    it was for a month
    Looking back as an adult
    Their relationship
    is what they hoped to work on
    At the time all I could imagine was
    a month was about as long as the whole damn summer
    We drive up to the woods
    about 45 miles from our home
    but another world to me
    Arriving with an enormous red plaid flannel sleeping bag
    a metal canteen for water
    a towel
    my dad's duffel bag from his Army days

stuffed with my bathing suit
tennis shoes
shorts
jeans
and numerous shirts for the stay
I settled into the wooden cabin I had been assigned to
and threw my belongings on the metal framed cot
The goodbyes
and the rest of the day are hazy
I remember the early daylight hours vividly
At eight years old
I still wet the bed
unfortunately
cotton flannel sleeping bags absorb liquid
yes
even urine
and they do not wick it from the body
I woke in the pre-dawn hours
wet
stinky
and
cold
It's hard to say whether the smell of urine
or the smell of shame was stronger
looking back now
it must have been a draw
No one
and I mean no one
said anything
Thankfully the other children didn't tease me
but they had to have smelled it
The counselor never said anything or even asked if I was okay
I went about my day pretending that I didn't reek
later when the horse I had dismounted stepped squarely

and fully on my foot
planting it there with no intention of moving it
I winced back the tears and swallowed my pain
all of it
the shame
humiliation
and physical discomfort of having an extra thousand pounds
resting on my small eight-year-old foot bones
That night I crawled back into a pee smelling
cold
wet
sleeping bag
and proceeded to pretend to sleep
This was pretty much the new nightly routine
my shame over my inability to control my body
outweighing the common sense of telling a grown up
who would have easily washed the sleeping bag daily and
resolved the problem
So
for thirty nights
I slept in that
cold
stinky bag
pretending that everything was okay
Yes
there were activities
yes
I had fun at times
Now I can't help feeling sad for the child who was too embarrassed to speak up on her own behalf
and kept up that mode of operating in the world
long after camp
My daughter once asked why I didn't report it to my
teachers

when I had soft-balls lobbed at my head every day in the 7th grade
I replied
My shame was greater than my impulse to stand up for myself
Now
I speak up

BUCK CREEK

I hate you
    he screamed as he slammed the wooden tennis racket
    into the three foot wide brightly patterned pillow
    He was venting about his mom
    I was a nine-year-old sitting in the corner
    small hands wrapped around a cup of coffee with as much sugar
and cream as I could get away with
    without the adults calling me out
    I was trying to stay invisible
    It was called an *Encounter Group*
    and was the 1960's definition of a midlife crisis
    There was a lot of yelling
    nudity
    and self-indulgent whining
    from my little girl perspective
    The next day warm and sunny
    a volleyball game began in the common area
    behind the conference center

A group of nude adults took both sides of the net
I slightly grossed out from the bouncing floppy body parts
headed back towards my cabin to read
or poke my eyes out
I don't exactly recall
I do recall thinking that there was no way I would ever bring
home any *Notices to Parents* from school anymore
they were not responsible grown-ups
That night I watched as a woman
who claimed to live in an old ice cream truck she had remodeled
talked about her life
She said she made her living by stripping off her clothes and
when the session got deeper
she proceeded to put on a song and slowly undo the buckles of
her overalls
twirling them to the lyrics
they call me mellow yellow
Flo was her name and she was chubby
which I could see
and kind
which I knew with my *spidey* kid senses
It turns out that she was the one to save my brother
My little brother had put his cozy red sweatshirt into the laundry
room washing machine after being told that it was filthy and had to
be washed
What his sweet seven-year-old self didn't know was that a red
sweatshirt could
and would
change the color of his father's underwear
and everything else in that load of laundry
pink
Besides changing the color
it changed dad's mood

and my brother got scared

Later that day he was told by dad that they were going on a hike

Towards the top of the trail

they came upon a small cabin structure with a man outside

The two men got to talking and dad shared the episode of the laundry

I'd spank him

I'd spank him good

said the cabin dweller with a creepy smirk

My brother recoiled and hugged the slope

staying far from the steep drop-off area of the trail back down to our cabin

Dinner time and the sun is still high

the adults still high

some of them

My brother started to walk in to the community building to get dinner and was stopped by the *Cabin Man*

You have to be naked

ask your parents

he said twice

Running on those tiny legs towards the cabin and the pocketknife his grandfather had given him

my brother was followed closely by the leering creep

Hitting the worn

wooden stairs of the cabin

just steps ahead of the creep

heart pounding

my brother heard

Hey

what's going on

They both turned to see Flo standing there

hand on hip in those faded overalls

a look of concern

like a mama bear
My brother looked at her as his hands shook
holding that small pocketknife his grandfather had given him
and finally exhaled
Mellow Yellow quickly became my favorite song

GO FOR IT

The photo hangs in her entryway
    It's a black and white photo of Martha Nishitani's modern dance
class in the 1960s
    Last month
    she came home loaded down with packages and bumped into it
    causing it to fall to the floor and crack diagonally across the image
of her in class
    It was a class of five and six-year-olds
    lined up across a wooden dance floor
    in black leotards
    The camera caught the students jumping in midair
    most of them
    a few inches off the ground
    hands up or to their sides
    but not her
    She is twenty inches above the floor
    knees bent back
    ankles tucked under her rear
    arms outstretched

as if reaching for the stars
Pure joy
or bliss
Happiness in a black old-fashioned leotard
with thick
white
underwear
showing at the side
Years later
her brother photoshopped the underwear out
knowing it had been a source of humiliation that day
As a child
she was embarrassed she didn't have the pale pink tights the other
girls had
and instead
she had strong
slender
naked
legs
He gave her the edited copy
and now as an adult
she prefers the original
The cracked one on her wall is the original version
and she hangs it with pride
Every day as she enters her home
she is reminded of that little girl
who
even though embarrassed and shy
let loose and was open to joy
jumping higher
and with more enthusiasm
than anyone else in the class
It always brings a smile to her face as a daily reminder to
go for it

LEMONHEADS

They came in a cardboard box and were sour and screamingly bright yellow

    She thought she was my friend because she bought them for me in third grade

    She was a Jehovah witness and was not allowed to pledge allegiance to the flag every morning as the class all stood

    hands on hearts

    at our plastic desks

    She was not allowed to dance

    She never celebrated her birthday

    Her name was Wendy and I liked her anyway

    She never could satisfy my curiosity about why she couldn't celebrate Christmas

    Because Jesus wasn't born in December didn't seem a good enough reason to me

    Just celebrate in June

    or whenever

    Duh

I did go to her house to sit in her room and listen to records on her
portable record player
   the one that may have been supplied by Satan
   I didn't ask
   I just know it felt sneaky
   and somehow very right
   For some reason
   she was allowed to come to my house to celebrate my birthday
   I hope she knows I loved her
   for more than her Lemonheads

SUSPICION

The art camp is an hour from home at a local university

    I am in seventh grade and have agreed to go but I'm not thrilled

    Ballet will be my major focus for the week

    I have only taken ballet for a few months at the Odd Fellows downtown on Saturdays

    I am nervous about fitting in

    We pull up to the university and look around at the dorms

    I will be sharing a room with my best friend Sarah and am curious if she's here yet

    Walking around the campus

    I try to imagine being a college student here some day

    The large hall is where we will eat all our meals

    and I can see the theater building across the lawn that holds the dance classes I will be taking

    Sarah has been my best friend since I moved into the neighborhood two years ago

    She kindly befriended me after watching Robbie Donnelly throw a pretend joint at my head in English class

    leading to my humiliation and giggles from his friends

The joint was a rolling paper filled with pencil shavings from the sharpener on the wall

It was clearly a pre- meditated move on Robbie's part and looking back

exactly the wrong way to get me to like him

I had never seen a joint and was mortified that he had flung drugs at me

Sarah stepped up to me after class and asked me to hang out at her house after school

I was grateful for the gesture not realizing until years later

that we were the nerdiest girls in our grade

Hugging my mom and dad goodbye I find Sarah and settle into our dorm room

Classes are okay but the teacher announces that by the end of the week we will perform a ballet for our parents

As she continues to talk

my stomach gets tight but I stuff it down and proceed with the steps

I glance over at the mirror

we look so gangly in our black Danskin leotards with our spindly legs hanging out

hair fastened tightly in buns secured with bobby pins

It's Friday night and our new friend Karen is in our room bemoaning how unfair it is that we only got fruit for dessert at dinner

Talk turns to raiding the kitchen

Creeping down the stairs in our long nightgowns we enter the dining room

Should we do it

I ask

Yes Comes the reply

We gently push open the metal swinging door with it's window just above eye level and proceed almost on tip toe

What's in the fridge

Sarah asks no one in particular

Forget the fridge look what I found

I point to a counter against the far wall

Three shallow aluminum pans each the size of a coffee table are lined up

we can smell the scent of chocolate before we even reach them

Where's a spatula Asks Karen

We don't have time

just use your hand to grab a hunk and let's get out of here before we're caught

I reply

The next day at lunch

a nun in full habit

crucifix hanging around her neck

clears her throat and addresses the cafeteria

We were going to have brownies for dessert today but somebody broke into the kitchen last night and stole them

The person who did this needs to confess or they will end up like Richard Nixon and go to hell

Sarah looks at me clearly distraught at that thought and whispers

We should tell

No

I whisper back harshly

If they knew who it was they wouldn't be saying that

We got away with it

COLTS

High school
    I envied those black patent leather high heel boots
    the ones that make you feel sexy when you walk
    Mine were brown leather
    heels slightly too high for me to perch atop with authority
    It was Christmas of our freshman year
    Your older brother bought you a fuzzy purple wide brimmed
fedora that would have given Prince wet dreams
    if only he was on the scene back then
    Your brother knew you well
    He knew that you would never choose the path of a button-down
PTA mom
    but instead would branch off and heed the call of your wild
artist's soul
    The song Radar Love came on the radio in the back seat of your
uncle's Lincoln Continental
    He drove up Ravensview Street as
    you
    Tricia

and I
sang along
giggling in that wide back seat
Half honored and half embarrassed to be seen in that car
we kept our heads down
We knew how cool we really were in our fifteen-year-old bodies
awkward as colts finding their legs
and just as anxious to do so
for then
we could RUN

DAYDREAM RANCH

1977
　　Kathy's house Friday night
　　Aerosmith Rocks album cranked loud
　　woofers blown
　　Apologies to parents the next day
　　Three girls working on their tans in the sunshine by the river
　　I place my hand just below my belly button and feel the concave
bowl that is my stomach
　　Hip bones gently rise
　　the natural formations of this pristine basin
　　White arms supine at our sides
　　We laugh about our arm bellies nicknaming that soft tender flesh
opposite elbows
　　Her parents are easy
　　Dad is a brilliant physics professor with all the social nerdiness
that seems to come with that
　　Mom the cool one who ate acid in the 50's and wouldn't judge us
if we smoked pot

The Red House
a bungalow on the property
was our spot
The boys from West Linn
the girls from The City
Rick tall and dark
in white corduroy jacket
wafts of Jovan musk cologne
Beer and weed
wandering into fields
chasing
running
waist-high grass
tumble
stare at stars
eager mouths touching
Rick's best friend the football hero
eating red pills to come down from the day's buzz
We
the city girls
ballet during the week
beer in the fields
feeling dangerous and grown
no adults
a whole ranch
loud stereo and the power of our bikinis
Mornings full of cleaning horse stalls
feral cats scatter from shovels
but those nights in the fields
oh those nights in the fields
under stars
musk cologne
and our hormones

chased away the smell of horse shit
every
time

THE DAY I GOT DUMPED AND FELL IN LOVE WITH GEORGE MICHAEL

Oh George
    my George
    I fell in love with you that Sunday as we drove past my best
friend's house
    I used to do ballet and argue with her brother in that house
    Her mother fed us in that house
    Now almost twenty years later
    I am listening to you on the radio
    in front of that house
    And
    I hear your voice
    your fear
    your courage
    We drove through the neighborhood to enter the freeway
    I don't recall where we were headed
    I do know that just before the freeway ramp
    he turned to me and said
    I can't be your husband

In retrospect to his credit he followed up with *I can't be anyone's husband*

Those words did little to anesthetize the ache that hit me in the gut as we picked up speed on the on-ramp

All I remember is throwing his ring at him

across the stick shift

Enter George

I listened to you on the way back that day and decades later you still echo in my mind with sweetness

Thank you for your vulnerability

Thank you for being honest and ripping up the world to be true to yourself

Thank you for honoring that faint cry from your heart

As I looked for meaning in the love I had lost

I saw something deeper

I needed a song of pain

of love

and fear

and ultimately

of strength

It takes a sensitive soul to see another

I found you George

II. FRIENDS, FAMILY AND LOVES

TIARAS AND DEVILED EGGS

Tiaras and Deviled Eggs
 she proclaims with enthusiasm
 in response to my question about what we should have at Uncle
John's Celebration of Life
 She is a tall wiry girl of ten
 long strong legs and light-brown hair down past her shoulders
 She who notices details
 preferences
 and what a person loves
 their
 passions
 We are planning a party
 a celebration
 a fiesta
 I met John as his employee
 and soon became family
 He worked full-time
 helping protect children from abuse
 and then spent from five to midnight

running a sweet little Mexican restaurant called Vera Cruz
Named after his home as a boy
he filled the space with antiques
love
and large vases of gladiolus flowers in bright scarlet and fuchsia
We hosted diners from all over the city
and often Darcelle
the owner and talent of
the longest running drag show bar in town would pop by for
dinner before the show
with his long-time companion Roxie
John was known for his big heart
love of beauty
and habit of seeing the best in everyone
At the end of each night the whole staff would sit around the
kidney-bean shaped booth in the corner of the dining room
and eat together
John's rule was the first glass of beer or wine
and whatever you wanted to eat
was on him
He always had a garnet colored glass of Rioja wine
a small strip steak
and enchiladas with red sauce
I always opted for the spinach enchiladas verde
This was an extension of his day job
helping bring people together and heal them
On the weekends
the discussion would often end with plans to go dancing
or head to the corner piano bar to catch some live music before
heading home
If the restaurant was cozy
it was merely an extension of his home
He had a 1912 four square house
large with a basement

main floor upstairs

and attic

The rooms were not only decorated

but curated

with art antique pieces

and seasonal Christmas trees or floral arrangements

John would have gatherings where

he would greet his guests at the front door of the large porch

and usher them into the living room with cocktails and food

The children got candy or other treats

and anyone who wanted one

could have a tiara

The backyard had quilts on the grass for reclining

and one year

a croquet game was set up through the hostas and pink flamingos

Yes

tacky things were always appropriate

In winter John's Christmas tree was difficult to see under the
copious amounts of aluminum tinsel

Some years I helped dress the tree with the hollering of

Throw more

more

more

you can never have too much tinsel

John made everyone feel comfortable

always anticipating what they may want or need

When the children were gone

the music would crank

and the wigs and tiaras would be out in full force

I always opted for the blonde bob wig as the incense was lit

Frankincense would waft through the house

with a swinging incense holder acquired from Father Don

a priest friend in Chicago

They had been in seminary together before John realized that

he could affect more lives
and live more authentically
by leaving
Although John was never ordained
I think Jesus would be proud
tiaras and all

THE DAILY SHUFFLE

It's five am and time for my daily shuffle
    from the blue and white striped couch
    heavy with blankets in the living room
    to the comfort of our king sized bed
    for a couple hours of better sleep
    as my husband leaves for work
    This early morning dance has been going on for 6 months
    with no end in sight
    I now recognize that
    neither of our needs are being met
    and the respect we once had for each other
    has whittled away over the years from
    disappointment
    and bitterness
    It is too late to fill the cracks
    they run too deep
    and are too numerous at this point
    Later as the subject is broached

it ends with
We can't afford
to
be
divorced

A NEW DIRECTION

A friend recommends I make an appointment to see an intuitive she's
been to
        and I show up at the appointed time
        Alana greets me in the waiting room
        where I sit focused on a large painting of a crow behind the
        reception desk
        I have been drawn to crows since I learned that they make tools
        and are highly intelligent
        I like their bluish black shiny feathers
        and keen eyes
        Alana leads me down the hallway to her office
        filled with small figures of Kwan Yin and Buddha
        two comfortable looking chairs
        a red oriental rug
        and a box of tissues within arms reach
        She asks me to draw three cards from a deck sitting on the table
        between us
        They are similar to tarot cards
        but with less defined

more abstract
art on them
She gives me a loose interpretation of the past
present
and future
and then shares the image she sees of my husband and I
growing more distant
and hostile to each other
Oh Megan
you are an artist
I see you standing in front of one of your paintings
in an art gallery
she states
You must be mistaken
I am not an artist
I reply as I tear up
Her words validate a tiny voice in my heart
I am just telling you what I see
You are clearly standing in front of your own work
in an art gallery
You may want to think about taking a painting class
she responds
Taking Alana's words to heart the next morning
I look online at local community college art courses
The only painting class that fits into my schedule is '*Painting II*'
and is at full capacity
When I show up the first day
I tell the teacher that I have no previous experience but need to
paint
and want to take his class
Welcome
he said
That one single word was huge
I doubt he will ever realize the impact his one word made on me

The term's assignment is to choose a subject
and do at least one painting a week around the same chosen
theme
Being drawn to urban landscapes
and having a proclivity for the often unseen beauty in
rust
and
corrosion
I choose an old yellow water tower on the downtown riverfront
Trying to paint in the rain with a clear shot of the tower is
becoming increasingly frustrating
and as I tell this to my teacher
he admits that particular water tower is his favorite as well
He suggests that I paint from my car
instructing me to put a sheet or large towel over the steering
wheel
and prop up a framed canvas against it
Pulling into a parking spot
with a clear view
I shut the engine off but leave my music on
I realize
today is the anniversary of the death of my dear friend John
and I insert a Johnny Cash CD
His deep gravelly voice is picking at the scab over my heart
Shit
now my tears are echoing the water on my windshield
and adding to the problem
of seeing my water tower
Johnny Cash is always cathartic
and seems the perfect soundtrack for this
yucky
gray
day
There is nothing like sinking deeply into the pain

and allowing time to just hang out there
with no judgement
or obligations
After a few tracks
I arrange a large beach towel over the steering wheel
and set a paper plate with dabs of fresh paint on another towel on
the passenger seat
I begin with the sky
It is gray and chalky
with my creamy yellow tower
defiantly
guarding the river
As the weeks go by
my paintings get progressively more abstract
ending with the one I title
The Conversation
It features a crane
with a wrecking ball
hanging precariously over my beloved water tower
As we talk about it during the class critique
I get clear that it is about far more than the water tower
it is a self portrait
and I need to make a major life change
This class
and my teacher's reception of my blossoming work
is inviting me to step into my OWN light
and give myself permission to be called
an
'artist'

THE SHIT HITS THE FAN

Missy Higgins' song *Where I Stood*
    is playing on the radio
    as I sit crying
    in my 4-door mom car
    I just dropped the kids off at school and started up the car to go
    Her voice singing
    I don't know who I am without you
    all I know is that I should
    I let the car idle
    and sit hunched over the wheel
    Tears come rolling
    and my only thought is
    she
    is
    me
    I let the song finish
    and call the radio station
    The DJ Actually picks up
    and I ask her what song is playing

She answers
and through my sobs
I ask
Who is singing
she is singing my life
I think I need to leave my marriage
thank you
Twelve years later
I listen to the song
Again tears come
but this time gently
slowly
and with a melancholic sadness
but
without the sting
They still ring true
and she still portrays so perfectly
the pain of knowing that things must change
and that it will hurt everyone
But now
on the other side
she does love him more
than I could
Not more than I did
when I married him
I was deeply in love
but more than I could
moving
forward

HOMELAND SECURITY

Funny how a small piece of metal can protect a human being from
poverty
    isolation
    lack of love
    A thin veneer of protection
    security
    a guarantee
    The myth we perpetrate
    and repeat to our young
    I watch in middle years as couples barter away dreams
    and passions
    all gone for the facade of permanence
    only to end up a holograph
    Hiding
    in a vacant broken chrysalis
    dreams having flown south
    a whisper of themselves at twenty
    A friend shows me a photo of an engagement ring

and without thinking
I blurt out
shiny handcuff
Oops

BIRD GIRL

The whispers can no longer be stifled
  Echoing against the walls of her heart
  they gain velocity
  determined to break free
  at any cost
  Inked crow on white shoulder
  offers to lead the way
  taunting her to open the cage door
  and fly
  She accepts
  Falling softly
  landing in a gentle nest of open hearts
  she submerges
  allowing the warmth to seep in
  through pores
  down to her marrow
  Her heart cracks wider
  with every beat
  pain trickles out

slowly
Parades of new friends throw
pink
orange
and purple confetti
that waft down
through the air
and
patch the crevices in her heart
with color again

CONCUSSION

An old-fashioned bottle opener pierces a triangular wedge
    deep into my palpitating heart
    The same heart that fed us both
    Pain drizzles out
    We share the same blonde locks
    and hard exterior shell
    Pride and joy radiate off his body
    until he hits the ground
    release
    release
    release

PICK UP THE DAMN GUITAR

Recently I was talking to a musician friend about creative expression
and how we can get out of our own way in order to let it through
   As human beings
   we are creative by nature
   it is an integral part of our biology
   This doesn't mean that we all express it in the same manner
   Einstein played with mathematics
   Picasso with paint
   My friend brought up the subject of Punk Rock
   He is classically trained
   but prefers writing and playing guitar in the rock genre
   He appreciates a finely composed song
   and spends hours on lyrics to get them just right
   This made it feel even more out of character when he blurted out
   Sometimes you must be a Punk Rocker
   just pick up the damn guitar
   Don't worry about it being 100% skilled
   or sure of yourself
   Just do it

with bravado
The Sex Pistols didn't let fear
or lack of musical training stop them
I had to laugh and agree
There is wisdom in getting out of your own way
to allow the creative process to happen
After all
We are conduits for expression
Just go pick up that damn guitar

MOTHER'S DAY

Large
    round
    head
    smiling face
    especially after eating
    Quiet by nature
    more sensitive than the dolphins
    you tried to let me know without words
    I was too scattered
    You so in tune
    and yet tuned to a chord
    I failed to hear
    I tried
    I really did
    but fear in all her trappings
    got in the way
    I will love you to my grave
    and
    beyond

MY LOVELY

She calls me my lovely
    which is quite great
    Her clear blue eyes show a strength of will that
    since birth
    reveals an understanding beyond her years
    She measures with compassion
    and insight
    in the flicker of a glance
    Always crawling off the picnic quilt
    to find those who look and act differently
    she has been a world citizen of the heart since infancy
    Blessed with the gifts of
    expression
    compassion
    and a deep reservoir of love
    she is
    my treasure

DAD

I saw his email title:
    Your art is a treasure
    I am seen
    He sees me
    Eyes suddenly fill overflow
    slowly at the edges
    Words of appreciation
    One artist to another
    Parent to child
    Acknowledgement of dormant talents
    Unspoken truths rise
    being witnessed
    Hidden treasure excavated
    after years underground
    Curated into a clear reflection
    of her souls message

III. SAN MIGUEL

MY TEACHER

I get up early
    after a fitful night thinking about writing down bits of my life
    and go to Mega Cable to sign up for Wifi
    to get a home phone
    It turns out that the 400 pesos that I already paid them
    was not for October (as I was told)
    but a fee to turn on the wifi and phone
    This turns out to be the beginning of a relationship filled with
frustration and misinformation
    I fantasize about laying down on the floor
    and having a tantrum screaming
    YOU LIED TO ME
    at the top of my lungs
    Feeling cheated
    but resigned
    I walk to the Biblioteca(library)
    I'm craving a library card
    so I stop at the check out desk

and hand them my ID and the equivalent $6.oo dollars They
photocopy my picture
    laminate it
    and hand me my official card
    This gives me permission to check out three books at a time
    One large wing of the library is filled with books in English
    Many of the ex-patriots from the US and Canada
    have donated both books
    and money
    to help fund the Biblioteca
    and it truly feels like the heart of the city to me
    A new friend teaches a music program for local children
    while the parents meet at the long wooden table
    to engage in open conversation in Spanish and English
    Walking into the open courtyard with round tables
    I notice a gray haired man tutoring a teen in the courtyard
    We begin a dance of eye contact looking away and then sun
glasses being put on removed and applied again
    This continues for 20 minutes until I look over at Elena
    who's patience seems to be wearing thin
    I head over to the check out desk and ask the woman behind the
counter if the man in question is a tutor
    She walks over to him
    leans down in conversation
    and then comes back to tell me yes
    he says he is a tutor
    I wait until his pupil leaves
    and then head over to inquire about tutoring me in Spanish
    I am Alijandro
    how are you
    he asks
    I am Megan
    and I am well
    how are you

I respond and ask him if he would be willing to tutor me in
Spanish

and we agree to meet at this table at 10:00 am next Monday to
begin

Today is the first meeting with a wise Aztec artist

who is disguised as my tutor

I walk up to the Biblioteca

and find Alijandro waiting patiently at the large wooden front
door with the other patrons

His profile and gray hair remind me so much of an old friend
of mine

he feels familiar

We go in together and sit at the table where I first spotted him

He asks me about myself my career and reasons for being there
and then proceeds to tells me the Spanish words for these subjects

I tear up as he asks about my reasons for being in San Miguel

I answer his question of why I am there with explaining how
unhappy I've been and that the United States feels so angry

Since I've been here I've only heard three children cry

and have not yet seen anyone visibly angry

I am taking a break after my divorce

and reassessing my priorities and life

I am here to paint

and experience the culture

At this point it is impossible to look at him and speak these words
without crying

He asks

Why are you so sad

I explain that my heart longs to live in Mexico

that I feel strangely like I have come home

and am frustrated about how to continue this long term

He talks about how full of rage the US seems to have

and we agree on how dangerous that anger is

He asks me if my husband was angry

and I tell him that it seemed that
he always vibrated with anxiety
We talk about our children
and he shares that his son is named after the Aztec god
Teotihuacan
explaining that the Conquistadors heard Teo and thought it
meant god
but really
it means warrior
He unpacks a backpack full of his paintings
and wooden sculptures that he is taking to a gallery that repre-
sents him
I ask to see the gallery
and we gather up our things
and walk across the street
and up Calle Mesones towards it

INSIDE HE SHOWS me a large painting of an Aztec warrior
guarding the Coming Age starting December 21st
I nod and tell him that I am aware of this event
The warrior has an upside-down heart between his legs
(like he is giving birth)
and he explains
Your heart must be open to enter the 'New Time'
A row of moons and other symbols line the upper edge and sides
and his signature painted like a tarot card is on the foot of the warrior
He is from Mexico City
and his blood is Aztec
It seems that I have engaged a teacher for much more than
Spanish
Alijandro is telling me
Kill the Ego
Thank those who have wounded you

and move on
they are dead in your mind
You are a strong
smart
woman
and it is time to move forward
No more crying
It is time to be happy
You can do whatever you want to
Oh my Aztec warrior friend
ever the teacher
and always cutting to the bone
Gazing through the cast iron swirls of my Juliet balcony railing
I look down at the street below
and feel caught up in the web of human activity
sticking to the web
like a spider
gladly
as I savor a sense of connection
I hear chanting
the deep vibrations of drums
and brass instruments
I run to the window to see a parade turning the corner onto my
street
It is crazy how elated I feel to be in this rich juicy culture
Gone are
my job
apartment
car
and more importantly
relationships that no longer nourish my heart
All that remain of my treasures
are packed in the hearts of a handful of people in Portland
and a 9'x12' storage unit

I am a rain soaked WASP
who has finally allowed my deepest desires and creativity
to surface
with freedom from judgement and restraint
Walking down the streets
I look everyone in the eye
and am amazed at the beauty and kindness I receive back
There is a gentle slowness
and reverence
for the human condition here
The lessons of love
kindness
and patience
are the ongoing themes
and this warm
golden
brown
country
is my classroom

AZTEC WARRIOR

Blood of the Aztecs courses through his small dark body
    Silver hair
    and a slow quiet knowing
    His patience for tears
    and the pain of others
    is endless
    and his wisdom profound
    He speaks of jaguars
    the night
    and things that are unseen
    We talk of cleansing our hearts
    and the stars
    Hired to tutor me in Spanish
    he instead tutors me
    in life
    His wisdom today
    When you can look in the mirror
    and see yourself
    really see yourself

you will know that you do not matter
we are all one
and your heart
will
shift

OUR LADY OF GUADALUPE

Our Lady of Guadalupe Day starts the night before
    at 2 minutes before midnight
    with exploding fireworks
    and the bells of the Parrochia ringing loudly
    Walking stealthily along the flat roof top of my apartment
    I stop to drink in the golden glow of the dome of
    La Immaculada Concepcion
    and the spiky
    rose colored elegance of the Parrochia straight ahead
    The bells finally subside at 12:25 am
    but the fireworks continue throughout the night
    and into the morning
    It is a cause for much celebration here
    I wake at 8:30 and read for a bit
    relishing the softness of my cotton pillowcase
    the weight of the blankets on my body
    and how lucky and grateful I am
    I fall back to sleep until 11:30
    Up and showered

I head to Buen Dia Cafe
where dishes were flying the other day
(Judith my favorite server tripped on the stairs above our
table and
sent dish fragments flying down on our heads like rain)
I order a BLT and Americano con leche as Elaina walks in
She joins me
ordering enchiladas verde
and Juan Carlos the owner
gives me directions on how to catch the bus
to the next town for the celebration of Guadalupe
*Walk down Calle Canal to Calle Guadalupe and look for the
chicken shop*
The bus stop is across from there
he instructs me
Elaina and I catch up over breakfast
and she wishes me a good day as I go to celebrate my love of
Guadalupe with others
Across from the designated chicken shop
I wait on a small dusty wooden bench
next to an older Mexican man (Jose Antonio)
who is juggling a bag of
Coca Cola
fried pork rinds
and a beautiful sheet cake
for his daughter's Quinceanera
Traditionally
it is considered the right of passage
from childhood
to womanhood
We board the bus
and I offer to carry the pork rinds that are trying to make
their way
to the ground

but as I'm asking
the cake goes tumbling to the ground
We climb the stairs
and take our seats
chatting in simple words
until he has to get off at the next market
to buy another cake
I continue to Los Rodriguez (supposedly a 15 minute ride)
but really more like an hour
After bumpy dusty roads
I spot the dome of the church
and I am dropped off on the side of the road
about 4 blocks from the center of town
I walk past stands of spun sugar cotton candy
pink and blue carnival animal rides
and then proceed along an avenue of
churros
pizza
corn dogs and
assorted meats that I am not aquatinted with
I am here to experience everything
but first
to the church
The church is clothed in flowers
Huge white Casablanca lilies
deep scarlet red roses
and dark green palm leaves
doubled back on themselves in loops
adorning the arched doorway
Entering the church
I see a huge image of the Aztec goddess/Catholic virgin herself
The amount of foliage and flora around her
but more profoundly
the sweet humid scent of lilies and femininity

is intoxicating
I choose a seat down in front on the right side
and watch the faithful come forward
some leaving a donation
and all drawing a card
They stare at it
as though it is a fortune from a Chinese take out cookie
with wisdom for their future
I move toward the alter
and put a donation in the basket
and draw my card
They all have Guadalupe on the front
and a photo of the church and a prayer on the back
I tuck this away
a treasure symbolizing my journey
from writing a college paper on her years ago in Portland
to standing in mindful presence at the end of a pilgrimage to my
love for Mary
and her Aztec cousin
I genuflect and pray
Please open my heart
and allow me to give and receive more love
Please open the hearts of my children
and allow the same
Please help me to be open to possibilities
and less afraid in life
Walking back out into the bright sun
I see tables set up with images of Our Lady on various items
I ask one of the young priests
Quanto Questa
and point to the framed picture night light
He replies that they cost 20 pesos for the small
and 40 pesos for the larger wood framed ones
I select two small and one large

all with red light bulbs and Guadalupe's image framed behind glass

He bids me farewell saying
Go with God
I wander on
stopping up the block
to watch the indigenous dancing going on across the street
Elaborate black and white feathered head dresses
colorful loin clothes
and moccasin footwear adorn the dancers
It is getting late in the afternoon
and I ask three police officers that are standing near a wall
for directions to the bus stop home
They point down a lane and start laughing
Okay I think
it's make fun of the gringa day
I politely follow their directions a few minutes before giving up and
turn back towards the church
heading over to the table where I bought the night lights
the young priest asks me if I need a refund or a trade
I lower my sunglasses to reveal my tears
and he and his brethren immediately take pity on me
I dig through my bag to get a pen and paper to request that they draw a map
He sees my face and says
No
I will take you
He takes my elbow and escorts me to the edge of town
stopping the bus driver
he asks him to take me to San Miguel
kissing me goodbye on the cheek with another
Go with God
I immediately decide my new mantra in Mexico is

When the cops lie to you
go to a priest
I realize that I am scared
it's getting dark
and without money for a motel
or a good grasp of Spanish
I feel vulnerable
As I exit the bus I have a deep sense of being home
It's nice to be back in what feels like my town
where
I have an apartment
friends who know me
and
a sense of belonging
Walking around the corner from the bus stop
I head into Los Milagros and order a taco salad and margarita
This culture fucking rocks I think as I chat with Francisco my
new friend who waits tables there
It feels like we are all on the same team
no better way to say it
maybe it is because of one dominant religion
or maybe the history of oppression
but I am continually blasted with the realization that this
culture is
so civilized
The small moments are truly celebrated
To prove this point further
I am walked safely home complete with a hug goodnight
The ever present church bells toll again announcing the hour
Something in the clang of the metal
reverberates through my heart
and seems to strengthen my body
forte
forte

as Aljiandro would say
Just 18 months ago
I saw no way out of a life that no longer suited my soul
now
I am I am nourished on a daily basis by this
warm
patient
culture

MY FAVORITE DOCTOR'S VISIT

Walking through the door
    past a drab waiting room of metal chairs and a red vinyl love seat
    more a bench from a van
    than real furniture
    I enter the exam room and sit down nervously
    As I describe my flu symptoms
    he looks at me with deep brown eyes that lock onto mine and asks
    Has art lost importance in your life
    Huh
    My brain responds silently
    This is brilliant
    Why don't all doctors ask this
    Talk about serious mind-body connection
    Reflecting back on this doctor visit
    I am reminded of how important art and creativity are
    to the human spirit
    This indigenous man from the heart of Mexico
    reminds me of what it is to be human

with one
short
beautiful
question

PRETTY

We met across a crowded bar
    He was the prettiest man I'd ever seen
    Jaw symmetrical and strong
    brown bedroom eyes glinting with kindness
    The tattoo on his back
    extending from arm to arm
    and down his waist
    Christ's head tilts to the right
    his mouth open as if in a moan
    Ink echoes the form of the living man
    I watch him sleep
    struck with sadness over the little boy in him
    who lost his father to a bullet
    then endured high school with the killer's son
    He is not the first man I've known to have such a tragedy
    and when he calls me spoiled a few weeks later
    I get it
    I had a family

a safe bed
The blue baseball cap hints at the boy-like charm
the white freshly ironed shirt
hints at the man

NARCISSUS

Ah-Haaa
   he says drawing it out
   in a cadence not my own
   I say Ah-ha
   It's short and gives equal weight to both syllables
   Neither is wrong
   just different
   Mateo's seems like the Mexican sun itself
   drifting into eternity in that second syllable
   Dressed in tight leather pants
   long black hair trailing behind him
   a parade of one
   he walks through the bibliotheca from his show of large paintings
   He is an artist
   a beguiler
   and very much a lover
   yet somehow always alone
   It is intoxicating to be held up as a goddess by this famous man
   virtues revered by him were never seen by my ex- husband

Being courted
flattered
and welcomed into his circle of artists and musicians
all with songs written for me
poetry and celebration was part of the pattern
before the fall
No sense of decelerating
it went from wild adoration
to cast aside in cool fashion
as if a garment change
Watching his ex-lover across the bar
I imagine introducing myself
exchanging stories with her
She
small
dark haired and stylish
in her tailored brown wool suit
so different from the constant sundress and sandals that have
become my new uniform
I'm guessing we would have similar tales of
a man getting bored
after just weeks
needing his constant life-support of fawning and giggles
I save my breath

CONFESSION

Languid shadow of Cathedral in pink
    Worship at the baptismal font
    Walk down the nave of repentance
    in search in the rectory
    Pray for forgiveness
    of what
    I'm not sure
    Priest probably twenty-five
    A figure cut from Vogue magazine
    Absolves without knowing what
    in a language we don't share
    After all he is obliged
    I walk away with redemption
    and impure thoughts of him
    After all
    I am not so obliged

MATADOR

Compact and handsome
    his life on the line in a visceral and profound way
    Forced to follow this path since adolescence
    a pride of heritage
    Tight gray pants and beaded bolero
    embroider the ugly truth beneath
    Scars cut deep
    Stitches down both thighs
    across the abdomen
    narrowly missing his aorta
    The beast tried unsuccessfully to save it's life
    by taking his
    His body a map
    the lines carved by
    fear
    horror
    and adrenaline
    on both sides

READY TO QUIT YOUR HUSBAND

Are you ready to quit your husband
    This came out of my friend's mouth recently
    as she described some of the issues that arise with our clients
    Oh Kat
    that's funny
    the phrase is:
    Leave your marriage
    not
    quit your husband
    I replied
    This is one of the many things I love about my friends who speak
    English as a second language
    Every once in a while
    the turn of a phrase is so different that it stops me in mid-thought
    and
    in a beautiful way
    redirects me to look at the same thing
    in a completely different new light
    We quit our jobs when we are miserable

realize that we have changed
have a desire to go another direction
stop playing small
follow our passions
This simple turn of phrase
quit your husband
equates it with a career change
subliminally giving permission
for it to be an option
to the woman contemplating it
What an interesting way
to take the emotional charge out of it
and examine it
under a different light

MEETING MAGGIE

Walking along the main road out of town past the art galleries
 I turn left and head down a dusty dirt road that follows an arroyo
 (a dry creek bed)
 It is lined on one side with a graffiti-stained cinder block wall
 Empty crushed water bottles
 coke cans
 and bits of candy wrappers
 litter the dry creek bed
 I turn right and then take a left down El Pial looking for her
house
 A petite energetic woman
 with a blonde bob
 large brown eyes
 and endless energy
 She opens the security door saying
 Buenas Tardes I am Maggie
 I introduce myself and we step into the kitchen
 which overlooks a bright blue swimming pool

a long deep yard
with two reclining chairs in front of a vivid purple wall
bleached bull skull
hanging above from a nail
Her attention to color and detail echoes my own aesthetic
and she leads me through
The Aqua Room
The Moroccan Room
and
The Violet Room
Mary says her bedroom is the Moroccan one
I am welcome to use either of the others
or
use one as a painting studio
and the other to sleep in
She continues
stating
I have naked margarita swimming parties with my friends some-
times and my hope is that you would feel comfortable doing the same if
you like
Oh Maggie I like you already
She leans down and picks up Cha-Cha
a sweet little fuzz ball of a dog
that likes to cuddle
and chase the pigeons that circle the pool for sips of water
Maggie hands me the schedule of the
pool man
gardener
and two different maids
the days they work
and how much to pay them
We agree that I should come the day before she leaves
to get keys and go over the alarm system

I smile and give her a traditional light kiss on the cheek
saying *Buenas Tardes*
and head out the front gate grinning
Who knew she'd be gone just a few years later
I really hope heaven has Moroccan arches and purple walls

EL DIABLO

Flat black eyes
    one blind since birth
    the other just as scary
    An unreadable fortress
    behind which vestiges of cruelty
    leak oily
    through veneer joints
    You speak about your daughters
    how you spoil the one who looks like you
    and verbally pick on the one who resembles her mother
    Tonight you tell me that you hit two dogs with your car
    Were they okay I ask
    Who cares
    they are street dogs and were fighting
    you respond
    The horror movie in my head begins
    and instinctively
    I shut up
    and push the automatic garage door control down a

round my heart
to the closed position
Definitions of sociopath
float through
as my primitive brain goes into autopilot
A small voice inside the garage warns me to
act normally
as I stare straight ahead
through the windshield
counting the minutes
until I board the plane
without you

HEART WIDE OPEN

The glance from a dog shoots in
    and a small cry is heard
    It echoes and reverberates
    against the red canyon walls
    bringing down small pebbles
    until they avalanche
    into thunderous boulders
    shattering her place in this world
    and cracking her wide open
    into universal love

WOUNDED

Best friends with addictions salve the moment
    drunken artists
    with sweet
    but rancid charm
    only go so far
    Seduced by this town's beauty and magic
    we gather and hunker down for relief from life's pain
    in this
    small
    cozy
    bar

VOYAGE TO THE STARS WITH TOAD MEDICINE

It is 6:30 and just starting to get dark as Valaria and I flag down a
    taxi and head to meet the shaman
    The car winds through a neighborhood
    filled with boutique hotels and large elegant private homes
    We are greeted by the shaman's girlfriend Anastasia
    who is Canadian
    speaks English
    and is quite gracious
    The home has been donated for the week by the owners
    so the shaman can do his work in town
    We are led through this oasis behind walls
    to a back patio living area complete with couches
    rugs and a tropical style roof of reeds and wooden slats
    I take a seat next to a quiet woman on the sofa
    facing away from the house
    Several ex-pats are mingling
    and I wonder if they will be there
    when I get my turn to journey
    The thought of having this experience with an audience

is making me uncomfortable
A few minutes later
Salvador the shaman
comes over and introduces himself
He takes my hand and leads me back through the house
onto the front lawn just inside the tall protective wall
The others all walk past and take their leave
we are down to four
Anastasia and Valaria discreetly sit near the house to oversee
We begin by standing in the grass
and I ask to have the harsh outdoor security lights turned off
Salvador tells me to look up at the stars and beyond
as he moves energy down my body
his hands placed a few inches from my skin
he starts chanting
rattling musical instruments made of nut shells
I stand with my ams at my sides
palms up in a stance of quiet receiving
He stands facing me
holds out a small glass pipe
filled with dried toad venom
instructing me to
first exhale deeply
then
inhale and hold it
I do as he says
and count
one
two
BOOM
His face fractures
into jagged
jewel colored fragments
my legs can no longer hold me upright

He holds me up
embracing me
saying
not yet
I am immediately in deep space
surrounded by blackness
and the light of the stars
I hear a deep universal voice speaking
Megan
You are dead
This is your last lifetime
A flash of recognition
The feeling
Oh
I really am dead
that's how it happens
In one moment
It overwhelms me
followed by
I am not enlightened
why would this one be my last life
I let the thoughts drift off
feeling connected with the whole of the universe
I am part of god
and
god is in me
and
in everything
WOW
A clear image of my maiden name in angular lettering appears
and I watch as it breaks into sharp shards and falls away like
icebergs
into the sea
Oh

of course that name feels so patriarchal
and no longer fits me
I am glad I listened to my intuition and removed both my maiden
and married names
The message is
It's all god
and your intuition is
how you access it
I come to
on my back
with moonlight gleaming down on me
I feel cool grass between my fingers
and notice a statue of Saint Francis to my right
Salvador reaches for me gently saying that it is time to get up
I have no idea how much time passed
When I emerge
I feel as though every cell in my body has gone far into space
and then come back
but in a completely different order
I tell him
it is like a computer file
the old program is gone
the new one is very slowly downloading
I'm not ready
I went very far away and the pieces are not fully back in place yet
it may take awhile
He agrees saying
Yes
yes you did
I have no idea how much time passed before he is there again a
second time
helping me up
I tell him
you need to hold me up as I walk

He guides me back to the patio and I sit in the same spot where
we had begun
Anastasia brings me water
Within a few minutes
Valaria begins her journey
and I am able to witness her experience
She is sobbing loudly and retches several times
About 25 minutes later
we are both sitting back on the couch with Anastasia
I do not remember anything except the deep voice
the shattering of my name
and Salvador's face
I turn to Anastasia
and ask her what she witnessed during my experience
She relates that
at first
I smiled
then cried briefly
then beamed with joy
and once I was on the ground
Salvador twisted and contorted my torso
while rocking and patting my body
My interpretation is that he was squeezing out old patterns
of thought and belief much like a sponge is wrung
to release dirty water
It truly felt like I died
and had been reborn in a different configuration
Valaria is next to me and takes a few minutes to drink her water
before we walk
wide-eyed through the house
and back onto the street
giving hugs of gratitude as we depart
The luminous night sky
and moon bathed cobblestones light our way

as we walk down the hill and under a huge stone arch
We head towards the huge glowing pink church in the main
square
stopping at a bakery on Correo for a chocolate cupcake to share
The whole thing has only taken a little over an hour
It seems such a small amount of time
for such a life-altering experience
but then I realize
most life-altering experiences do happen quickly
It feels too soon
and I feel too vulnerable
to be alone in my small apartment
so Valaria invites me over for gooey grill cheese sandwiches
and to talk about what we each experienced
I share with her the voice I heard
it's message
and images
She reveals letting go of things that have been holding her
back for years
and I give her my experience of the wringing sponge
An hour or so later I walk up Calle Relox to my place
After a fitful night
I return to Valaria's the next morning to continue trying to figure
out what exactly has happened
She tells me about an upcoming meditation with Tibetan sound
bowls that is supposed to be profound
We make plans to meet at 6:15 in the evening
and walk down to the holistic center together
Around 4:30
the weather turns to pissing rain
and the cobblestone streets turn into canals of
quickly rushing water
By 6:00 I find an old black windbreaker
with corroded zippers that will not close

and my red cowboy boots
Neither are very waterproof
but the boots are a better alternative to my flip flop selection
I grab two bed pillows to use as seating
and shove them under the jacket
like a pathetic Santa Claus
A taxi drops us off about a block away
and we follow other rain soaked attendees
down the winding alley
past the large brightly painted Guadalupe on the wall
A large psychedelic painting greets us in the foyer
and I whisper to Valaria
If I stared at that during our session tonight I'd be transported to the stars again
Well
it turns out
I didn't need an image of the virgin to send me to the stars again
I enter the meditation room
arrange my pillows
and lay down on the cool tiled floor
As I stare up at the cupola ceiling with it's hole in the center
I can see the night sky
and reflect on my journey of the night before
Once the group has assembled
the leader welcomes everyone
and gives a brief introduction to the evening
He explains that we will begin with
quiet meditation
flowing into sound
with Tibetan bowls
a didgeridoo
and an accordion type instrument
that is played by opening and shutting it like a suitcase
He announces that the evening will conclude

with chanting and drumming
As soon as the Tibetan bowls start
my body begins vibrating
It starts in my
feet and hands
and then moves to
my ears and the
sides and back of my head
My feet feel as though they are moving about
8 inches from side to side
I start getting really scared
I look down
to make sure my feet are still there
The voice in my head starts coaching me to
stay calm and grounded
but anxiety is winning
The leader begins blowing the didgeridoo
and it intensifies until
I start seeing the stars
and moving towards them
as my body
melts into the universe
I am leaving my body
and this time without the aid of any substance
I'm scared that I may not come back
Shit
At least Salvador was a shaman
and medical doctor
I do not want to call attention to myself
but am afraid
I feel like I need intervention
to stay in my body
I call out to the group
I'M SCARED

HELP ME
Immediately Valaria has her hands on my back
and the woman on the other side of me is touching my leg
Tap on my
right
then left
harder
I demand
I bend my knees up
and put my bare feet flat on the cool tiled floor
and start pounding them into the floor
first one
and then the other
until I can really feel them again
The leader comes over and continues with the Tibetan bowl
until I shout
STOP
THAT'S
MAKING
IT
WORSE
He stops for a few minutes
then begins chanting
continuing with the agenda of the evening
It takes about 20 minutes for me to feel fully back
and as we conclude
I ask about the didgeridoo
He explains that it is used to achieve altered states
Well it sure works
I reply
(My smart ass sense of humor seems to have returned)
We all wander out into the hall to put on boots and rain gear
and head out into the night
Sleeping has become a huge challenge

every time I start to fall asleep
I feel a sense of falling into space
(as if off a cliff)
and the intense fear
that I am dying
At one point
an intense
electric-like shock
in what feels like
my heart
along with an audible
ZAP
sound
jolt me awake
The sound is like a mosquito
hitting an outdoor bug zapper
but amplified
This scares
the shit out of me
and I lay awake
in a state of anxiety
The fear becomes so overwhelming that
I turn on my laptop and start watching movies for distraction
The normally comforting sounds outside my balcony of
drunken revelers and music
is sending adrenaline rushes through me
I'm in a
hyper-anxious
hyper-aware
state
that leaves me feeling
cracked wide open
on edge
and

vulnerable
I keep seeing tracers when I move my hands
and every
sound
color
and
form
is amplified
The hours from 2:00 am until dawn are the worst
but then those always seem to be
The next morning I call Fernando
He is working but tells me to meet him at Cafe Monet
so I throw a dress on and hoof it quickly down the hill
I walk in towards the back and see them at a small table for two
As I approach
he pulls up another chair
and introduces me to his client
They finish their meal
welcoming me to come along with them as they run errands
While his client is in the lumberyard
I sheepishly ask if I can stay a few days with him
telling him how terrified of the night I have become
and how I need to be around someone
in case I freak out and have to go to the hospital
I accompany him home
and stay a week as he
cooks
calms me
and
has his
large
sweet
pit bull
sleep on my feet

to anchor me in my body
I watch TV as a distraction
to the dark abyss
that night has become for me
I feel like a small child
and his unconditional support and caring
is one of the nicest things I have ever received
Back in my studio I settle in again
and reclaim my space
It feels good to be back in my neighborhood
and I swing through the Jardin to sit on a bench and people
watch
and feel connected before my afternoon appointment
The counselor I found is an expat from The States
who has also journeyed with Salvador
and I feel like she is the perfect person to talk to
about my ongoing sensations and fears
Her office is on Zacateros Street and up a steep set of stairs
behind a beautifully painted door
We spend a little over an hour as I tell her that
I'm afraid I will die soon
She asks
Do you think you will just be walking down the street
and drop dead
Yes
actually I kind of do
I feel like I have unfinished business in several
of my relationships
and I'm afraid to leave the planet just yet
Well
you won't
she responds
and then adds
The lingering affects should subside shortly

and that electrical jolt you felt to your heart
has been experienced by others
at the time of falling asleep
Since she has graciously gone over our time
I thank her and say goodbye
Descending down the stairs
and climbing back up the hill towards the main square
I walk past my friend's gallery
but they must be closed for comida (lunch) because the door
is locked
I want to talk to him about my experiences because
he had his own shamanic experiences with the native
Huichol people years ago
and had lengthy visions
I guess I will call him
once I get home

MAGNETIC NORTH

A cobbled street
    400 years old
    He walks by
    cocoa eyes lock with green
    The electricity is jolting
    Stepping backward from my door
    the gaze comes again
    and again
    twice more
    Extending his pointer finger
    he rotates it skyward
    curling it back
    towards his native body
    in a slow directive motion
    that forces me back to collide with
    magnetic north
    Hi
    my name is Megan
    I have just returned from the shaman

I think I am supposed to meet you
I say as I look into his eyes
Hola
I am Jesus
He smiles
Of course you are
I laugh

PARQUE JAUREZ

Grecian urns top crumbling pedestals
    Celadon water floats spears of palm
    catching ripples of light
    Small unseen birds squabble
    hidden by large tropical leaves
    Circular brick patterns hug the fountain
    The sound of basketballs smacking
    asphalt
    and chainsaws whining
    crack the air
    A couture couple from Milan
    walk hand in hand
    focused on their looks
    Local teenagers lean against antique pillars
    tongues entwined
    oblivious
    Americans walk pampered pooches
    alongside dirty
    hungry

street dogs
A skinny black crow
holds a berry in his sharp beak
staring at the gringa watching him
Cold cement
braces warm thighs
through my thin green dress
Kisses to friends
and slow savoring
farewell to San Miguel

IV. BACK HOME

STORM WARNING

Storm warning at sunset
    Pink clouds
    gray at the edges
    like wallpaper
    The smell of ions
    and a heaviness
    Damn
    She has two speeds
    Inspired enthusiasm
    or utter despair
    They interchange at a rate
    that is scary
    Enthusiasm usually wins
    Two babies
    they compete for nourishment
    Despair suckles quietly at her breast
    while enthusiasm overfeeds
    until too fat to rise to greatness

she rolls over in the mud
giving up

BUTTERFLY COLLECTOR

She collects men like butterflies
    Colorful
    and exotic
    pinned behind glass
    so they stay pristine
    Each a different pattern
    shape
    and species
    Combined
    they form a piece of the mosaic
    that fills the crack
    in her heart
    From various continents
    with different histories
    they quietly nestle tightly together
    as swifts do in a chimney for the winter

ACCORDION

I am an accordion
    I am made from something that was before
    Infused with new life
    Eager to express
    Sometimes expanding to fit the space
    breathing out
    infiltrating every last corner
    with the whisper that is my soul
    like a curl of smoke winds it's way to the ceiling
    Other times contracting
    pulling in those strong
    but delicate edges
    in order to simmer
    condense
    strengthen my song
    Duality in every moment
    breathing in and out
    quiet and loud

always
all of me

SPLAT

Moving too quickly causes her soul to ride the rim
    and spill over the edge
    losing bits of herself
    ounce by ounce
    She has trouble containing it
    in her tall blonde frame
    Grabbing hold of the nearest edge
    she re-centers
    and assumes the correct cultural position
    being sure to smile
    and act calmly
    The prescription states
    to balance the spirit
    which makes her smile
    The doctor asks
    So you feel like your spirit is
    spilling out of your body
    This simple question qualifies her to write such a script
    Walking down Davis street

she glances left quickly to avoid the skateboarder
and drops her parking receipt
Leaning over
she grabs it
Drip
A little bit of her overflows
like a glass of iced tea being knocked over
and again
more of her splats onto the sidewalk
Leaving one's body can be fun
but living like this sucks
Her transformation seems to last forever
but to date it is only 19 months
since smoking the Toad Medicine with the Shaman
Her intuition is heightened
and she is able to see patterns in new ways
which excites her
but the ongoing unbalance
is hard to camouflage in public
and is cause for concern
and embarrassment
The word Kundalini
meant nothing more than an abstract idea of sexual energy rising
until she journeyed to the stars and came back
her cells in a a completely different configuration
She is learning to adjust
and has teachers in old friends
who have the sight
Letting go and accepting this new path
is her vocation now

ALTER

Elk skin tight across birch hoop
　　Hawk feather and crow share the same vase gracefully
　　Mother Mary looks down
　　smiling from antique mirror
　　over white candle
　　personal mementos
　　and burning copal incense
　　Clear crystal rosary from Mexico hangs in the center
　　echoing in the glass
　　and blessing all that sit below
　　and are reflected by it
　　Sacred toad figurine hides red skull cattle cap
　　symbolizing the delicate veil between the worlds
　　Curved mahogany
　　and Italian marble stand
　　lay the groundwork for the offerings passed from church
　　to almost priest
　　to heathen
　　Holding sacred

both
Native
and Catholic symbols
she kneels on a pink velvet pillow
to touch them all and genuflect
in quiet reverence
and complete gratitude
Merging continents
dogmas
and symbols
until they unite
as a drum beat
echoing through her heart
and spilling out all over
in waves of messy love

TALISMANS AND TCHOTCHKES

She was my first
    Her sorrowful glance
    grabbing me from across the aisle as I walked past
    with my
    collector friend
    Just get her
    you can start a collection
    She said enthusiastically
    yet
    with a touch of boredom
    like
    you have to start somewhere
    And so began
    the collection of Marys
    The slow introduction of a porcelain figure
    that became a group
    and eventually ends with
    me taking her name
    both in the baptismal font

and
on every legal piece of paper I own
And
after all the years of adding to
and reducing
she is my first
and last

THE VEIL IS LIFTING

Frayed at the edges
    like a Tibetan prayer flag in the wind
    Patches worn thin
    moth holes allow the truth to peek through
    The veil is lifting
    It's always been this way
    Hidden
    Seen only by those looking
    at a certain angle
    and
    with the right heart
    The veil is lifting
    The truth is forcing it open
    Gouging holes
    with its urgent
    angry
    fingers
    Tearing the delicate threads
    ripping hard

violently
I am afraid
but I know
this needs to happen
The veil is lifting

INSIPID

The news
    social media
    newspapers
    and tv have always been so
    but now
    the odor wafting off them
    is that of
    rotting flesh
    Somehow
    the perfumed dryer sheets
    that have kept it palatable
    are gone
    and the putrid rot
    wafts through the nose
    into every pore
    and deep into the lungs
    creeping in
    and laying waste
    in the visceral cavity around the heart

The heart
The heart knows better
The heart knows that this garbage
is not the truth
It is only a form of waste
just like urine
The heart has no words to defend its stance
but if we listen
we can hear the echo of its wisdom
from beyond the ages

BAPTISM OF TERROR

I am keenly aware of
    the exact moment my body hit the water
    All I can think is:
    How big is this
    how could I have gone this long
    without knowing
    Now that I know
    the secret
    there is no unknowing
    It starts with tears
    progressing to sobs
    Scenes of Mexico
    and Italy
    scan quickly across my eyes
    Get away
    Run
    Run fast
    Run and bring your loves

Eyelids squeeze quickly
as the curtain comes down
it won't matter
our planet is a commune

MAKE WAY FOR CONDOS

Walking by
    I see gashes in her ribcage
    ripped away
    leaving huge splinters
    Wood and straw
    encrusted with plaster
    strewn about
    Raw
    she's exposed
    like open-heart surgery
    Chest cracked open
    and forced apart
    Wide open
    and vulnerable
    Her facade still a pristine painted porch
    welcoming guests with wicker chairs
    and a table designed for tea
    Perfectly good
    no signs of disease

she is being eradicated
erased
The new owner
so quick to destroy
so anxious to pretend she never existed
discarding
rather than re-using her organs for others
She is not alone
Her wise old tribe being discarded
replaced with young adolescents
crafted from plywood
and greed

CHARISMA

Moss green eyes hint at sly childlike mischief
    A sexy leprechaun
    A trickster
    The path you tread
    stone by stone
    grout still wet from
    the tears of countless women
    curing and binding them together
    Hardening as your story
    You float through the room
    A scent
    A vapor
    A wisp of smoke
    Curling over guests
    caressing shoulders
    cheeks
    and ears
    The big game hunter
    adoring those he's shot

Unlike mounted deer
the women are willing
feeling alive at the invitation
to once again
play with fire
He grooms women as a game she says
craftfully massaging
carelessly bruising
his specialty
Those who feel invisible
who have forgotten their true beauty
their own spark
Feigning interest
casually dismissing
he flickers
like a candle
when the door closes

SEXY SIRENA

Mexico is where I saw your heart
    fully come alive
    The rhythm of the day
    slightly slower
    everything slightly sweeter
    as if we were there
    to savor moments
    You grew up in a fisherman family
    me the newbie
    grew up in a family of nerds
    now shrieking as the tuna I caught
    flipped
    and
    hit my belly
    causing the boat full of women
    to explode with laughter
    Eating fresh roasted shrimp off large metal baking trays
    buying straw fedoras from Oscar
    who walked up and down the beach

with hats stacked high on a pole like Bartholomew Cubbins
we'd walk down alleyways
taking photos of the fuchsia colored bougainvillea
We wandered into art galleries
and sipped tequila with the artists
stopping to listen to musicians
and flirt with handsome locals with liquid brown eyes
It was salve for our souls
Being fully engaged
Admiring beauty
and creating it
As your body has left
I choose to imagine your soul residing on those beaches
laughing
laughing
laughing

WARRIOR GIRL

She is red
    Not a pale persimmon
    but a
    I am here and will get shit done
    kind of red
    A red that reveals heartbeats
    and courage
    Comfortable in her skin
    she glides from political cocktail party
    to homeless shelter
    and then under the hood of a race car the same shade of
    Bring it on
    crimson
    Taking in baby birds
    she nurtures all around her
    before gently blowing a puff of air under their wings
    as she invites them
    to soar

IN SERVICE

I want to be in service
 She turns her head and says to me
 I look into that clear blue gaze
 and take in a deep breath
 suddenly feeling calm
 For almost two decades now
 she has been one of my greatest teachers
 The first I can recall
 to keep me mindful of my language
 to point out the power of semantics
 to speak to how our words
 do matter
 Her frame petite
 graceful
 her presence on this planet
 huge
 Our work brings us together
 and apart
 like the in and out

of threads
on a loom
Able to stand alone
but so colorful when together
Growing up
I felt service was important
but as more of a duty
an obligation
boring
I didn't look deeply enough
I didn't see the joy
I now recognize that being an artist
a creator
an entrepreneur
can indeed be
being in service
and the results are huge
Sharing art
words
deep listening with others
brings immense joy
and gets multiplied
even squared
as it ripples out
and others feel inspired
I have gratitude for my friend
and the power of changing definitions

IT TRULY IS SHARING from our souls.

JOSEPH SMITH GOT YOUR TONGUE

You choose to play with hearts
  so cavalier as to pierce without gushing
  but nonetheless leaving a thin scarlet trail of pain
  that winds up and down valleys
  through years
  finally drying up without a word
  or whisper
  leaving sand pictures on the earth.
  I give you the benefit of fear
  with my mouth wide open
  in amazement of cruelty
  or ego
  or maybe just
  stupidity
  I've seen you open up to pain
  revealing your tender flesh white belly
  It was beautiful
  I hate to think it was for game
  maybe even sadder

to know you choose to close it up to fit in
and not fully live
Peace be with you
I sincerely wish
that is
when I'm not irritated with you
wishing once again
you would reveal your tender side
and live bravely
But
we all have free will

PORTRAIT

It is humbling to feel how much you love me
    You see in me
    the shiny sparks of fire
    that my others tried to dampen
    You revere
    and honor them
    to the point of creating art
    to hold witness to their flame
    and kneeling down with creaking bones
    to declare your admiration
    This gift
    is greater than any other

LISP

Today
    my lover told me
    that I have a lisp
    You have the same lisp as your father
    it's subtle
    but it's there
    He states
    Really
    I lisp
    How long have you noticed this
    I ask
    Since the day I met you
    and then when I met your father
    I heard the resemblance
    he confides
    Hmm
    I hum at him
    It's odd to start learning integral parts of yourself after fifty
    and

I am grateful for his observations and pronouncements
Do you think you notice it because
English is not your native language
I ask
I am still stuck on the fact that
all through my marriage and long-term friendships
over the decades
no one has ever confided this little tidbit to me

RELEASE

Raw ache
    Tongue languid
    now cool
    Dreams reveal shadows
    Soaring in the cathedral of my mouth
    wet cavernous hollow
    Echoing your name
    lips closed
    to savor
    one last taste
    before I let you go

DOVE

I accidentally broke my lover's heart
    exactly 442 days ago
    Tonight he brought me his leather jacket
    It had been my cocoon
    zipped to the chin
    between pajamas and sheets for warmth
    in the high Mexican desert
    Frayed lining
    shows signs of a past
    so much like my own
    It cloaked me in courage
    when I walked home at night
    over cobblestones
    bathing me in protection
    and a school girl's dream
    of her big strong man
    Yanked from me
    a desperate attempt to remove all vestiges of him
    that night he stormed out

Now it is brought as a soul offering
with bottle of red wine
and
a sweet kiss good-bye
I had the lining re-sewn
It is yours
He smiles
Our scabs still fresh
the gesture
a dove

SWAPPING PAIN

You were my transition man
    and I
    your last chance woman
    Never meant to be real
    the pain certainly is
    Past wounds were healed
    but
    unexpected fresh ones show up
    Need for connection and touch are met
    but the high is brief
    and the hangover
    cruel

MAESTRO

I see you at your window pacing back and forth
    your desk to the left
    heavy with papers
    Heavy with the responsibilities
    you choose to keep you busy
    Busy from examining
    Busy from deep feeling
    Busy from engaging deeply with those you love most
    I see you
    in your glory
    I see you
    the responsible one
    I see how they adore you
    You
    are the leader
    You
    are the master
    You
    are the wise one

My dear maestro
You don't see
we love you
You don't see
we want your smile
You don't see
we honor you
Even if you stopped today
Something inside you
tells you to keep going
Those who love you
wish you would pause
There is nothing left to prove
You truly are good enough

FORGIVE ME

Whisper to me lazy honey
    stop the bare beat of my heart
    Reveal cool thick dreams that lick at the weathered pink rust
    The underbelly of ships
    forced down by sirens
    moaning with love
    Aching
    unheard
    and gasping
    Salty water silencing screams
    Bitter drunken words lather and foam to the top
    Floating on the surface
    violet blue bubbles reaching out
    They pop in the early morning sunlight
    diluting and dissolving
    memories and pain
    All is forgiven
    Go forth

J.C.

A cocky arrogance covers the pain
    swaddling it
    keeping it safe and cozy
    A tattoo covered wall defends the core
    but crumbling mortar
    allows thin shards of sunlight
    to pierce through
    and illuminate soft spots
    Fear
    and an army of defensive soldiers
    keep the penetration
    to a minimum

BUT WHAT WILL WE DO WITH MOTHER

She was the eldest of three
    the first born of a minister's daughter
    and an engineer
    who was orphaned early
    Her mother was in charge
    Always on guard
    after all
    her mother's baby brother
    died at four from the flu
    which only proved
    that diligence to safety must be adhered to
    at
    all
    times
    In a home filled with *should* and shame
    sitting on her dad's lap
    listening to a story
    felt like luxurious respite from the stress
    Jean whispers into his ear as he leans forward to turn the page

Daddy
when I grow up
I want to marry you
Sitting up and smiling
he whispers back:
But what will we do with mother

VIOLATION

Walking up the stairs
    I see the bright blue of an IKEA bag at the furthest edge behind
    the house
    I pass the front door
    and grab the bag gently
    feeling a sense of familiarity
    as well as dread
    What is my antique trunk doing in the backyard plopped down
    next to the bag over-flowing with
    sports bra and undies
    squeezed between all my old record albums
    now damp and swollen
    A canvas army backpack stuffed with blankets
    sits like a colonel at attention
    watching over the scene from the gravel pathway
    Walking into the garage
    I see the bikes are gone
    boxes opened
    and strewn about

We raised our children here
creating gardens
cozy indoor spaces
a precious nest for our babies
That was twenty years ago
Now the collateral damage lays
like a gelatin overlay in an old film
covering our lives with a sepia stain
the damage
done by a stranger
uninvited and unwanted
Someone
or two
who felt compelled to enter our nest
pocket keys
rip through cupboards of baby clothes
my grandfather's engineer award
embedded in clear plastic resin
my children's artwork and toys
examined and discarded
with no thought
You leave me feeling violated
You have touched things dear to me
examining my life with no personal lens
ripping apart boxes of heartfelt art and memories
as if shopping for a deal at Walmart
I walk into my beautiful home to find an upheaval of my treasures
memories
things created from our souls
You used my new white towels to shower
scrub your dirt clean
your decision to take my poetry books
is a sign of your entitlement

As I gingerly use two fingers to pick up the wet
filthy towels from my basement floor
I see your used syringes
FUCK YOU
You stole my memories
my ability to feel safe in my own home
You desecrated my sacred space
I hate you
Picking up the bundles you left in my yard
I drop the note I wrote to you
my only way of feeling heard
my only way of confronting you
when you eventually skulk back
for the rest of
your score

YES QUEEN

I'm never visiting a national park again
    He proclaims in a high-pitched tone
    tinged with drama
    dripping with the sweet lure of gossip
    although the subject hardly warrants it
    Do you know how many people are MURDERED every year
    between Bigfoot
    and bad guys
    His friend across the table jumps in
    Oh my god
    have you seen the tv show about real people
    being killed on cruises
    It's CRAZY
    he screeches from atop his
    gorgeous
    black cashmere
    turtleneck

. . .

GENE SIMMONS *and KISS were on the Scooby-Doo cartoon*
  you know the tv show with the song
  Scooby Doobie Do
  I love you
  Once they took the makeup off
  they weren't that great
  I never really liked their music
  The five men are huddled
  at a picnic table
  on the deck of this spot
  known for its world-famous Rueben sandwich
  The place is owned by the former mayor
  who won in a landslide
  He is a bike riding rebel
  a human-powered bike
  not a Harley
  But what about all the buffets and nightly shows
  The previously quiet one utters
  almost under his breath
  and yet full of desperation
  As if on cue they all yell in unison
  Shows every night
  It's all I can do
  not to stand up
  arms high above my head
  and
  holler back
  Yes Queen Yes

SING ON THE BEAT THAT FEELS RIGHT

This week I got some impromptu tutoring in music structure from
    my musician friend
    He was tapping out the beats to a Neil Young song
    and I asked why he always did that
    He went on to talk about 3/4 time and 4/4 time
    and explained that
    most popular songs are in 4/4 time
    Once I got the concept of why
    structurally
    a waltz is different than Neil Young
    he continued by discussing the songs he writes
    Most times my vocals will come in on the first beat
    but in some of my songs I come in on the
    second
    third
    or even fourth beat
    depending on the feeling I want to convey
    You just start singing on the beat that feels right
    I've been letting this marinate all week

I am struck with the
profound meaning hidden in the off the cuff remark
and a situation from years ago came back to me
It was senior year of high school
the first day of a music appreciation class
The teacher was outlining the syllabus and explaining his grading
structure ending with
The final will be an oral report on the composer of your choice
NO
My brain screamed
I darted into my counselor's office
Mr Ryan told me the other electives were full
I would have to stay enrolled
I knew I would end up flunking
There was no way I was going to get up in front of everyone
After our grades came out
I was called back into Mr Ryan's office to talk about my grade and
how I could have done it differently
I couldn't do it
I couldn't stand up and give a report to the whole class
I was too scared
Megan
Sometimes you have to face the music
I don't know if he meant it as a pun
but it stuck in my head because
it was so unlike the way
my parents spoke to me
Just last year
a friend challenged me to write some poems
and speak them aloud at a local coffee shop
I told her that the idea both excited and
scared the shit out of me
So I would commit

and say yes
A few weeks later
I found myself in front of a group of
maybe eighteen or twenty people
Holding my poems
visibly shaking
but doing it anyway
This one act
felt incredibly brave
It led to sharing my work in other venues
and getting published with others from around the world
So many times
I felt pressured
to begin on someone else's timeline
but
I finally jumped in
on the beat
that felt right

FOLLOW YOUR HEART TO ITALY

It had been twenty-six years almost to the day when I returned
    Venice
    known as La Serenissima
    meaning the most serene
    stole my heart all those years ago on my honeymoon
    I vowed to come back someday
    A friend of mine is going through a divorce and has stopped going
to some of the places she used to go to with her husband
    She no longer felt safe there
    afraid of all the old memories of him
    the sadness it brought up
    We needed a mission to reclaim those spots
    We grabbed another friend of ours and went on a Reclaiming
Tour
    The first spot was a hotel with concert grounds
    We went to see Sheryl Crow and my friend danced and sung and
    left later that evening feeling reconnected and safe on her own
terms
    There is great power in that

An older friend of mine and I were talking about six months ago
he shared that an acquaintance we both know had recently died
They gave him six weeks
and he died in six weeks
I thought about what I would want to do
if I were given a six week diagnoses
I blurted out
If that were my diagnosis
I'd go to Venice
The next day I woke up and realized that one of my biggest
desires
was to go back there and I shouldn't have to wait for a reason
or make an excuse to make it happen
I figured it out and booked a ticket to Italy
I felt a rush in doing it
even a little fear
I hate to fly
(well really I hate the take-off and landing part) and multiple
take-
offs and landings just to get there felt brave at the moment
I could use a little brave right about now
Talking it over with my mother one day at lunch
she said
Oh
I completely understand
after my divorce I had to reclaim the beach town we used to go to
Do you remember the time we got those crazy photos taken in the
old western costumes at the beach
That is what I was doing
Reclaiming Venice sounds like a great idea
I went alone on this trip
it challenged me in ways I needed to be challenged
It gave me the complete freedom to live
in the moment

every single moment
and tune into the absolute beauty of my surroundings
I got teary as I walked off the water taxi from the Grand Canal
into the main piazza in Venice
She was just as gorgeous as I remembered
it almost literally stopped my breath
That night I met a gondolier
who was about to retire
and sweet baristas
in what was to become
my new favorite place
I was asked if I was Italian by three different people
including an Italian tour guide
which made me smile
From Venice I traveled by train to Rome
After standing in front of Trevi Fountain I walked into a church
stumbling into an ongoing mass
I sat behind a family with three teens who couldn't stop squirming
and their mama who looked to be my age and kept ruffling their
hair to keep them in line
She made them say
Peace be with you
when we grasped hands and
she realized I was an English speaker
It was sweet to see the playful energy between them
I felt like a child
so overwhelmed by the beauty
the history
and the beautiful ways that things intertwine
I was prepared not to let Rome get under my skin
but she did
Not only did I reclaim Venice
but I fell in love with Rome as well

Among my souvenirs are
new friends who live in London
a new sense of knowing that I can land on my feet
and an appreciation for new places
food
art
and culture

SENSITIVE SOUL

His arms are covered with thin pink lines
    laterally lacing across
    from forearm to shoulder
    A shy downturn of the head
    dark hair falling slightly
    as he pushes the spout on the bright orange Igloo water jug
    on the deck across from where his parents sit eating tuna melts
    My heart tugs as I see those lines
    wanting so much
    to lean over
    and tell him
    I can see his sensitive soul
    I want to tell him that it will be okay
    that when he's older
    maybe he can guide young ones
    who feel like he did
    None of us get out of here without battle scars
    some are just more obvious to strangers

A CRISP WHITE SHIRT

He walks into the courtyard
    Leading with confidence
    a crisp white shirt
    salmon colored sunglasses
    and matching walking shorts
    Designer flip-flops complete the look
    Three men already at the table
    greet him with smiles and enthusiasm
    I watch as two of them quickly dim
    Not a huge gesture
    just a few awkward side glances that reveal what's going on
    They are all handsome
    one slightly chubby
    one more grunge
    but all with sweet smiles and eyes
    In my mind
    I draw them all in crisp white shirts and designer shoes
    just to level the playing field

so they stop looking sideways
and just
project their greatness

FIRST DATE

She is somewhere between twenty and twenty-five
    her right arm is covered in an ink sleeve of images of pain and
    death
    The most benign one seems to be a tooth with blood dripping red
    dye down her triceps
    Above it is a coffin
    (shut thankfully)
    but with an eye crying and tears adorning the top
    A red skull complete with dripping blood
    a noose around it's
    neck glares at me from her left arm
    He arrived first and once she is seated
    orders for both of them
    rattling off soup
    salad
    artichoke dip
    and then pasta for her
    and a steak for himself
    His cocktail arrives

elegant with a sugared rim
This displeases him
he comments
pushing it away and ordering a beer
She orders a cocktail that arrives in an old-time
wide rimmed champagne glass
replete with flowers cut into the glass around the middle
It is the ghoulish color of a three-day-old bruise
Apropos of the tattoos
I ponder
If she lives to be ninety
will the images on her arms take on a different meaning

HOW SHOVING COFFEE UP MY BUTT SAVED ME

You just boil it up let it cool
    then insert the nozzle
    she says smiling over the table in this little brick café
Don't you know I have a tattoo that says Exit Only
On my lower back
I quip in response
Well it's easy and you will feel so much better she continues
You know it used to be in the Merck Manual that doctors use for
treatments
I'm afraid it will perforate my colon and
I'll go septic
and die alone
on my floor
with crap everywhere
Okay then don't do it
but really
it will be fine
I can tell that I am sounding neurotic

but
I actually am
a little worried
Just lay on your side on a towel on the floor
or if you prefer
in the tub
Wait about fifteen minutes
and then sit on the toilet and release it all
It's easy
She grins again
Will you call me an hour later to make sure I'm okay
I almost whine
If that will make you more relaxed then sure
she replies
Two days later
bucket and tubing in hand
I boil coffee
strain and cool it
and proceed to the tub
She has agreed to call an hour later
but I beat her to it
I feel
AMAZING
I yell into the phone
I feel all clean
and really shiny
I have energy
but not the jittery kind from drinking too much of it
and my intestines don't hurt as much
WOW
I keep babbling
I do the treatment a few more times that week
and

now any time my gut acts up
I promptly shove coffee up my ass
willingly

ANASTASIA

I call her Anastasia
    she is dark green
    compact
    and knows how to sit still
    I admire this
    She feels safe enough to sit with her back to me as she rests
    That feels rare for a hummingbird
    And I take it as an honor
    Her nemesis
    Bixby
    is larger
    with a hood of magenta sequins
    He dive-bombs her as she drinks
    perching on the round red ledge
    There is plenty of sugar water
    he is just
    an asshole

V. THOUGHTS ON AGING

THE SQUIRRELS HAVE COME

My mother is eighty-seven
    going on eighty-eight
    These last few years have been a series of Sunday breakfasts
    talking about squirrels pouring syrup on themselves
    and other such sentences
    that form in the brain
    when you no longer can hear
    and try to read lips
    Don't misunderstand
    she is still quite bright
    no dementia
    just fanciful interpretations of her daughter's sentences
    The worldwide lockdown situation
    has taken this humorous quote
    to one of complete frustration
    Yes
    most of us have the phone
    and online platforms that allow us to communicate
    but with the lack of technology skills

and her deafness progressing
these are no longer options
My mother was a teacher
a therapist
and an early childhood educator
She is truly one of the wisest people I know
Hands down this woman is
SOLID
That being said
it is enormously frustrating that at this point
She is sequestered up thirteen floors
We talk on the phone
but only get in a few sentences
before it becomes
squirrels in syrup
again
Just as I am trying to express my feelings
or share a sweet story
the curtain of deafness
comes crashing to the stage floor
in all it's
bright
red
crushed
velvet
opera- like
glory
I'm sure she feels the same way
but
because of either training
or her personality
she deflects
and starts down a different road
always keeping it light

onwards towards a better outcome
I recognize that my frustration comes
from knowing
we don't have much more time together
and
having restrictions imposed
just adds to the poignancy
My mother's mom
who lived during
and
had loved ones die
in the flu outbreak a century ago
Her little brother Francis
died when he was four
leaving my grandmother
with a prevailing fear
for the rest of her life
We are all trying to do our best to stay connected
Recently I was trying to help my mother fix her email
over the phone
when she paused
and said
wait a minute so I can put on my little old lady voice
I got quiet
and she came back on the line
in a high squeaky
almost Disney-like character voice
She said
Hi Megan
it's your mother
and I'm a little old lady who can't do computers
Then we both laughed
and she said in her normal voice
Well

I may not have email
and I'm losing my hearing
but at least I still have my sense of humor
Thanks mom
You truly are a wise woman

HEARTY STOCK

The phone call came last night at 8:07 pm
    from the head nurse where she lives
    This is Megan
    I answer quickly
    so as not to waste time
    and get to the point of what's wrong
    Your mother has fallen
    She's hit her head on a glass table
    and they can't get it to stop bleeding
    We'll have to call 911
    she needs stitches
    Do you have any questions she adds sweetly
    with that calm nurse tone
    No
    but I want to make sure she gets a CT scan
    I'm more worried about a brain injury than the wound
    I respond
    I'll let you know what hospital they take her to
    Okay thanks Cindy

I hang up the phone
My brother set up a nanny-cam when we moved her into this
apartment
there are two of them
one set up towards the hallway to see comings and goings
one on her desk
pointed towards the floor
between her favorite chair and the bed
We explained this to her
saying we wanted to monitor the floor area
to make she wouldn't lay there for long if she were to fall
She once was lying on the floor
for over three days
no one knew
she was unable to reach the phone cord
to yank it off the table
It came with bed sores
dehydration
and humiliation
Her mind and memory are still strong
at eighty-eight after being on heavy meds for rheumatoid arthritis
for over fifty years
she is resilient
She always told me
We come from hearty stock
I think it was one of the more positive things her mother told her
in her litany of shaming
I don't know if she remembers that the cameras are there
I'm almost certain she doesn't
last night when Cindy called
I logged in the replay
and watched a painful scene of my mother's walker
getting caught on something
her being propelled onto the edge of a metal table

then falling
crying gently
like a kitten mewing
help me
please help me
I watched the caregivers so sweet and compassionate
the firefighters arriving
trying to get answers
from a woman whose ears no longer work
I heard her say she was eight-four
actually she's eighty- eight
then some laughter
as her personality
and kindness came through
Hearty stock
seasoned with kindness
that will be
her legacy

PUSHING ON SHAME

This pandemic is pushing on childhood feelings of shame
  she said quietly through the phone
  Even though I am wearing a mask and staying far from others
  it brings up feelings of not doing things I should
  or not doing things right
  I feel like it's old childhood stuff
  and I suddenly feel
  4 years old

YOU LOVE WELL

You love well
  She says quietly into my hazy green eyes
  as I lean in
  an intimate gesture with my mama
  These days she proclaims
  anointing with truth
  and absolute clarity
  She was raised by
  the daughter of a preacher
  The last two decades
  she has declared that
  her soul is Jewish
  Since the mini strokes
  I feel
  she has become more of a
  Buddhist monk
  Food
  once a source of pleasure
  has lost its calling

no longer
a focus or treat
Meals are left
mostly uneaten
The awareness of
less time
a gift
Laser focus
on the moment
feelings
kindness
Horse blinders
block out
politics
drama
future plans
past experiences
We are this
This moment only
staring eye to eye
speaking directly
to the heart
You love well
She says again
I
her daughter
whisper back
Thank you mom
you taught me well

ONE STEP FORWARD

We
        are not the lead
        in this box step waltz
        Surrendering control
        over tempo
        and direction
        we try to remember to smile
        Directing workers and health care professionals
        we remove obstacles to falling
        organize daily events
        and
        try to interface technology with someone born
        almost
        a century ago
        She is lovely
        She is kind
        patient
        intelligent
        We

her children
are mostly the same
patience
being tested weekly
if not daily
Putting out fires
exclaiming
One step forward
two steps back
our mantra these last few months
We work as a team
my brother and me
Leading with love
we recognize that part of the surrender
is the awareness that
the dance will be over before we know it

GRIEF DISGUISED AS A LACK OF LEMON RICOTTA PANCAKES

As an introvert
    I get a sense of connection
    from sitting alone in restaurants
    and coffee shops
    writing
    reading
    or just having a meal
    briefly chatting with someone at the next table
    or stool
    I willingly wait over an hour in line
    to get
    my favorite lemon ricotta pancakes
    black coffee
    and connection
    banter with my favorite server
    picks me up
    the way a new pair of earrings might
    for someone else
    I woke this morning

my tenth week
of social distancing
and home
sequestering
to an enormous
overriding
sense of sadness
after reflection
I recognized it as grief
As the day progressed
I realized that I'm grieving over
the uncertain future of spending time in my favorite places
supporting my local eateries
meeting up with friends for meals
and the very real possibility
that way of life may have come to an end
at least in the easy
cavalier
spontaneous way
we used to enjoy
I currently live alone
many times during these last weeks
I've been grateful
for the freedom of my own space
the freedom to stay up as late as I want
sleep in
without interruption
and have no one to get on my nerves
That being said
phone calls with loved ones
can only go so far
I ran into a dear friend at Trader Joes last week
we both awkwardly started to go in for a hug
only to stop mid-point

perched on the invisible line of fear
a social no-no
His daughter whom I'd never met was with him
as was my daughter
it felt so foreign to not at least shake hands
or hug
He grew up with hugs
and such expressions of friendliness
we both felt stifled
As the weather turns to summer
my inclination is to turn toward the sun
I am painfully aware that this sadness
and loneliness is both
from lack of human connection
and lack of the connection of many things I took for granted
and
I now recognize it
as the little gemstones
in the jewelry box
of this
shy introvert

AN EXISTENTIAL LONELINESS

I need a tribe
    I have a tribe
    I have people who have loved me
    from before birth
    literally
    I have people who have loved me since
    I was a wee child
    climbing trees
    and proclaiming my truths
    I have people who have loved me since
    I was a gawky adolescent
    who never quite fit into my clothes
    or my body
    I have people who have loved me since
    I hated high school
    and rebelled
    through dress and action
    I have people who have loved me since
    I tried on different jobs

like hats
always excited at first
but ultimately tossing them aside
I have people who have loved me as
I settled down and married
becoming a wife and mother
I have people who have loved me as
I changed religions
got divorced
left the country and
ultimately
found my soul again as a grown-up
I have people who have loved me as
I navigate with them
through this upheaval
of old paradigms
and ways of doing things
I still have people who love me
What I now need is people who will still love me
if I speak my truth
I need people who will still love me
if I share my fears
people who will stay open enough
to hold opposing views without judgement
I feel like I no longer have a tribe
I feel the isolation of
having to wander out
find new people who will love me
in spite of
or maybe because of
my new beliefs
It ultimately will bring more love
It feels raw and scary now
I feel like I did on Kauai

when the radio announced that
a missile was coming
heading
straight
towards
us

PRIMORDIAL ACHE

The shifting mist gently rises from the pond
    up through the cat tails
    into the skirts of greenery
    surrounding strong evergreens
    Huge land formations remain after ions of shift and birth
    Stuck for now
    content to be there
    they allow rich green moss and lemon-yellow algae
    to creep up
    and claim their home
    Driving past
    I turn inward and proclaim
    finally
    this is my home

IN THE COMPANY OF WOMEN

There is a certain comfort
    A certain sense of ease
    Unspoken words
    and gentleness run through us like a breeze
    We share a monthly cycle
    a common language of our needs
    The depths of understanding that
    our bodies hold the key
    At once a gift
    and a burden
    to be
    the bringers of the light
    we fret
    and pray
    and wish
    that it will all turn out alright
    As maidens we do worry
    As wives and mums in strife
    we walk this path together

divining our way through life
As elders
we witness and hold
the sacred prayers of those who come behind us
gently holding their cares

STEP OUT OF THE SHADOWS

I see you
    I see that ray of light that you are trying to hide
    It leaks through and shines
    to those of us who
    take the time to look
    I know you take precautions to hide it
    so you don't get ridiculed
    or teased
    You take good care of that sweet little child inside
    You are such a great protector
    I know all these things because they hold true for me as well
    In middle school
    I had softballs thrown at my head after gym class
    every day
    by other students
    My perceived crime
    my parents not being able to afford more than 2 pairs of pants for
    the year
    I grew quickly

my pants always way too short
Where's the flood they would yell
I had no idea what they meant until I learned
pants that short were called high waters
not socially acceptable
I endured this daily until graduation
I dimmed my light
I got even more shy
stopped risking looking stupid
put my heart in protection mode
Decades later
I recognize the damage this did to my soul
It has caused me to second guess myself
doubt my intuition
stopped me from fully showing up with all my gifts to share
It is such a waste
I will no longer hide in the shadows
I will share ALL I have to give
shine brightly as the true radiant soul I am
and invite you to
do the same

A THREAD THROUGH THE YEARS

The deep sound of a train whistle
    more like a boom
    winds up towards my deck from the tracks by the river
    I'm on a different deck than twenty years ago
    but the train is the same
    Like a bright thread
    weaving through fabric on a loom
    maybe scarlet
    or crimson
    It makes its presence known
    and reminds me of both
    my fuck-ups and successes
    Years ago
    I used to drop my children off at school
    and sit waiting for it to cross my path
    daydreaming about gunning my engine straight into its side
    as it rambled on heading west
    I never thought about the carnage
    just how everything would stop

everything that was eating a hole in my heart
I loved my children
it wasn't that
It wasn't really anything I could put a label on
just a
deep
deep
sadness
Today I listen to its call
and think about how
I could have done better
Today I think about how
I can be soft with myself
for not gunning that engine
That train whistle is like a relative
a good friend
someone who causes reflection
and can measure progress

DOWN THE ROAD

I feel like I break your heart
    She says from her hospital style bed
    Her left lower eyelid is red
    and I have requested medicinal eye drops from the nursing staff
    No
    I don't feel that way mom
    do you say that because I'm teary
    I ask looking into those soft blue eyes
    I'm crying because your sister Jean
    is in her last few days before dying
    I respond
    I know she's not doing well
    but I didn't realize she was dying
    she replies
    She doesn't recall our talk from twenty minutes ago
    and doesn't quite get that Jean is hours
    or days
    from the end
    As my mother shares her heart

occasionally referring to a desk as a building
I kiss her goodbye
for now
See you down the road
She smiles at me as we say
I love you
and I walk out the door

THE TRUNK

How's it going
    Jim asks as he leans over the table
    His ruddy face clean-shaven
    eyes clear
    and steady
    Direct eye contact today
    rare in the past
    perhaps shyness
    Shitty
    I respond with a quiver
    My mom is in the trunk
    I choke
    I just picked up her ashes I continue
    Oh I'm so sorry
    He responds
    his tone with a note of sadness
    after a look of confusion
    I order a huge hazy beer
    and my favorite sandwich with extra cheese

Small bits of pleasure to soothe the ache
My sandwich half-eaten
I watch Jim as he touches the back of a slender man
perhaps in his thirties who has just come in
and is heading to a table across the room
It's a touch of familiarity
with a gentleness
like towards a lover
or dear friend
This place is my refuge
my seaside cottage
my mountain cabin
Its wooden beamed interior
and walls crammed with photos of past
and current patrons and friends add to its coziness
It's a family-owned venture
the owner was once the mayor of this west coast town
with his own brand of originality
a bicycle always at hand
and a loud
Whoop-Whoop
bellowing from below that gray beard
Legend has it
when he started this place in the 1960s
a bar fight broke out
which led to his mission statement
dedicating the place to
welcoming extremes of opinion
but stating
If physical violence is in your nature
either develop your verbal abilities
or leave
I brought my children here twenty years ago
playing checkers in the back booth

There was always a newspaper on the bar
games under the counter and
lively conversation at the tables
At the end of the bar
sits a veteran of Vietnam
his tee shirt emblazoned with the battleship he was on
He anchors the corner with a beer
and a story of those past days
for anyone wanting to talk
Another older regular sits on the patio in the summer
content to be in a sea of human beings
I come here to
write
eat
meet with friends
and feel welcomed as an introvert
with just the right amount of interaction
and alone time
The night after my mama died
after spending the day moving everything out of her apartment
and sorting through her possessions
I hunkered down at this place
Sitting at the bar
trying to hide in the far corner
tears streaming down my face
I was greeted with love by the woman who brought me a beer
and the cook who whispered to me that
she gave me all the best pieces of crab in my salad
sharing that she lost her dad a couple of years ago
and the pain still pokes through at times
As I finish my sandwich
Jim comes over to ask if I want another beer
He confides in a very uncharacteristic way
See that guy over there

He points to the table across the room
That's my brother
This is the first time he's been out of the house in six weeks
since he was in the hospital
and almost died
I'm so sorry for your pain
we never know how long we have
he adds quietly
So true I think to myself
We never know when we'll be in somebody's trunk

BEING

I can't be
  what you want me to be
  but
  I am happy with myself
  I am finally done with
  searching for the shine in another's eyes as
  I now see it keenly in my own
  I have come back home and
  am in love
  with the girl
  the wise one
  and
  the future crone I see
  I am tickled by the way she cracks herself up
  designs living spaces
  and
  on a grander scale
  her life
  all to be beautiful

and deep
Deep with the contrast
of ease and pain
love and hate
or almost worse
dismissal
I see the contrast of walking in this shallow world
always looking for the secret pool to dive deeply into
Oh to jump in
get wet with knowledge
wet with faith
wet with love
and all it's messiness
I love that beauty exists
It often seems
the only thing that truly matters
beauty in a smile
a tear
a longing
an answering
I love the scars
The scars on my arm
where my brother dug his nails in
when we were stuck in a car on a long roadtrip
The ones across my belly made by the grazing bullet
trying to take down this Wonder Woman
they run parallel to the one
lone
line
where life exited
against his will
pulled out by a sumo wrestler
dressed in nurses clothes
I have come home

LESSONS LEARNED

My aunt calls
    we agree to meet at my favorite cozy lunch spot on Broadway
    Elaine is at a small round table as I enter
    Kissing each other on the cheek with a quick hello
    I settle in and order a tuna melt and iced tea saying
    The last few months have been amazing
    I have learned so much
    She leans in and comments quietly
    You look really good
    you seem very different
    Do you want to know what I think it is
    Of course
    tell me the truth
    She holds my gaze and
    slowly says
    you lost
    your
    shame

ABOUT THE AUTHOR

Megan Saint-Marie is an author, artist, and coach.

For the last thirty years she has explored spirituality, religious practices, and her place in the world. She loves watching people and dogs, and talking about all things esoteric. Her writings speak of relationships through appreciation, pain, and humor, sometimes through a lens of snarky insight.

She has been published in an international anthology of poetry, online digital magazines, and has read her work on stages and the radio.

Her writings come about from her experiences as a mother, wife, friend, lover, and observer of people and patterns.

She ventured off to Mexico for a year to paint, write, pray, meditate, and ponder the universe.

She currently lives in the United States.

YouTube: @MeganSaint-Marie
TikTok: @writermegan
Instagram: @megansaintmarieauthor

instagram.com/megansaintmarieauthor
tiktok.com/@writermegan
youtube.com/MeganSaint-Marie